Earth Falls Asleep

Donna M. Tabone

About The Author

Donna M. Tabone is a retired teacher and first time author. She and her husband of 45 years have three children and live in Southern California. As a child, she loved reading and listening to a variety of stories and enjoyed the many characters she met along the way. That enjoyment blossomed into a deeper love and appreciation of Children's Literature. She appreciated most, those books whose authors and illustrators received the Caldecott Medal Award.

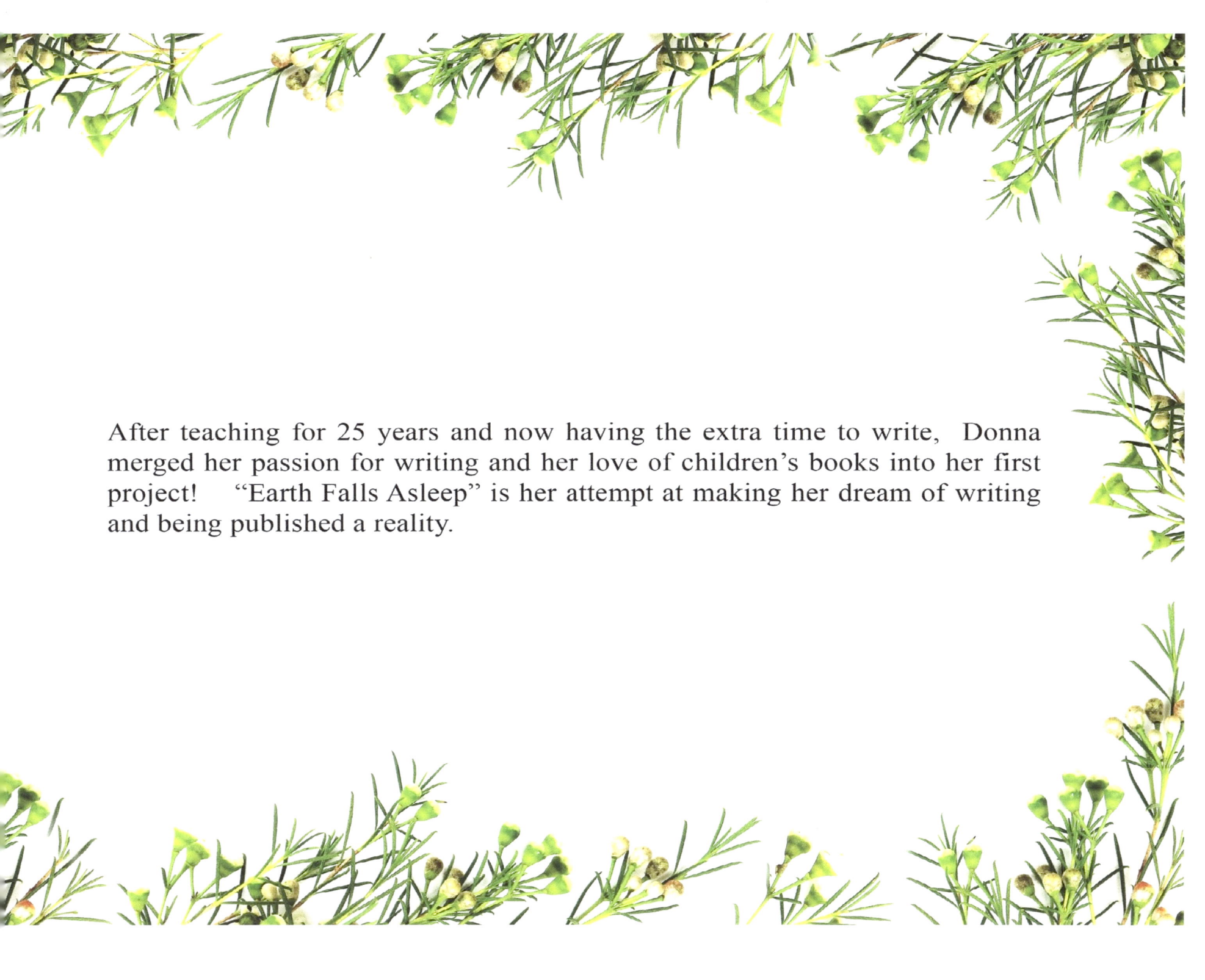

After teaching for 25 years and now having the extra time to write, Donna merged her passion for writing and her love of children's books into her first project! "Earth Falls Asleep" is her attempt at making her dream of writing and being published a reality.

About The Illustrator

Welcome to the mesmerizing world of Jason Green, a visionary fine art illustrator whose work breathes life into imagination. With an unparalleled passion for creativity and a keen eye for detail, Jason transforms blank canvases into captivating visual stories.

Born with a natural talent for illustration, Jason embarked on his artistic journey at a young age, honing his skills and refining his unique style over the years. His art is a fusion of classical techniques and contemporary flair, seamlessly blending traditional craftsmanship with modern aesthetics.

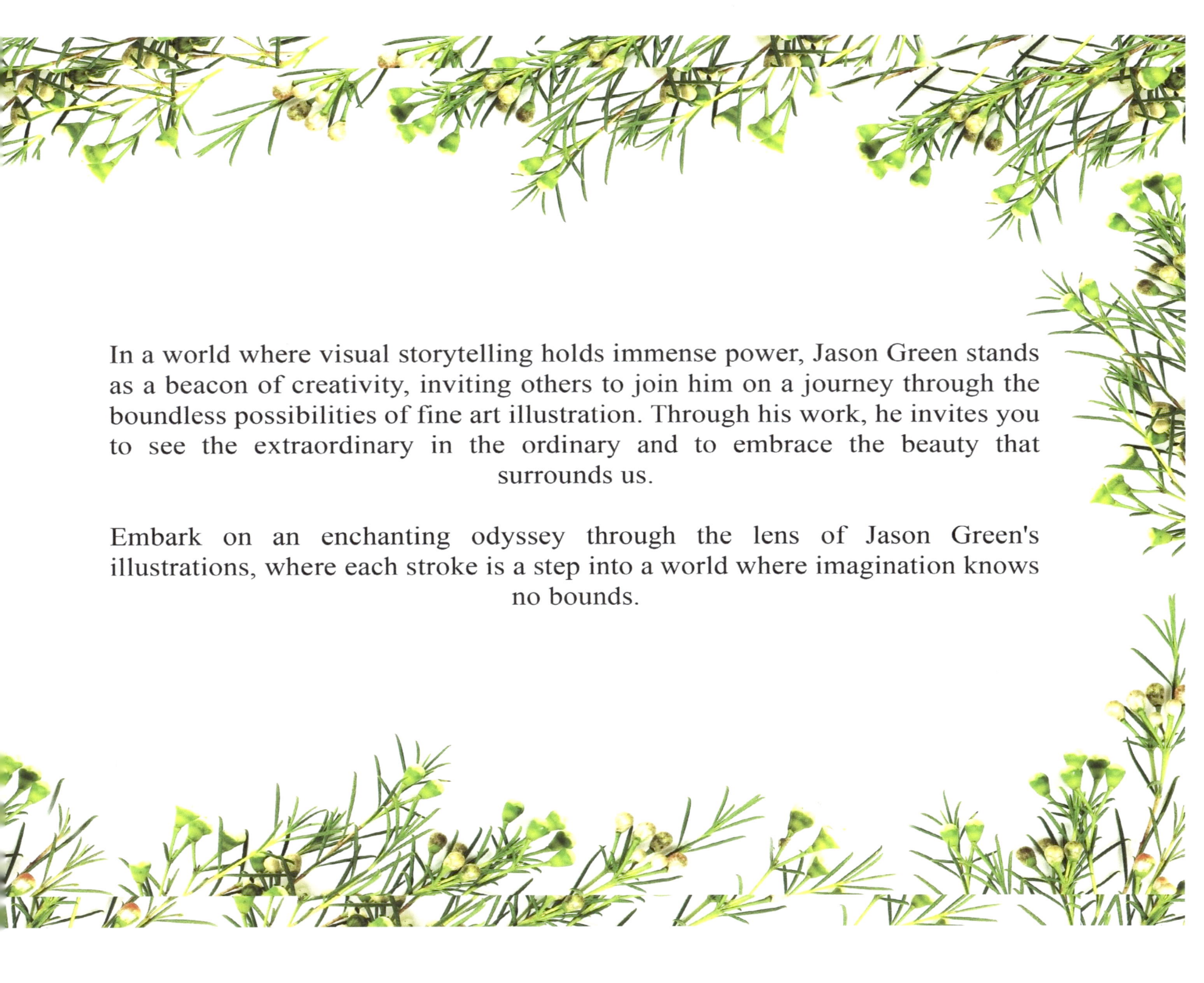

In a world where visual storytelling holds immense power, Jason Green stands as a beacon of creativity, inviting others to join him on a journey through the boundless possibilities of fine art illustration. Through his work, he invites you to see the extraordinary in the ordinary and to embrace the beauty that surrounds us.

Embark on an enchanting odyssey through the lens of Jason Green's illustrations, where each stroke is a step into a world where imagination knows no bounds.

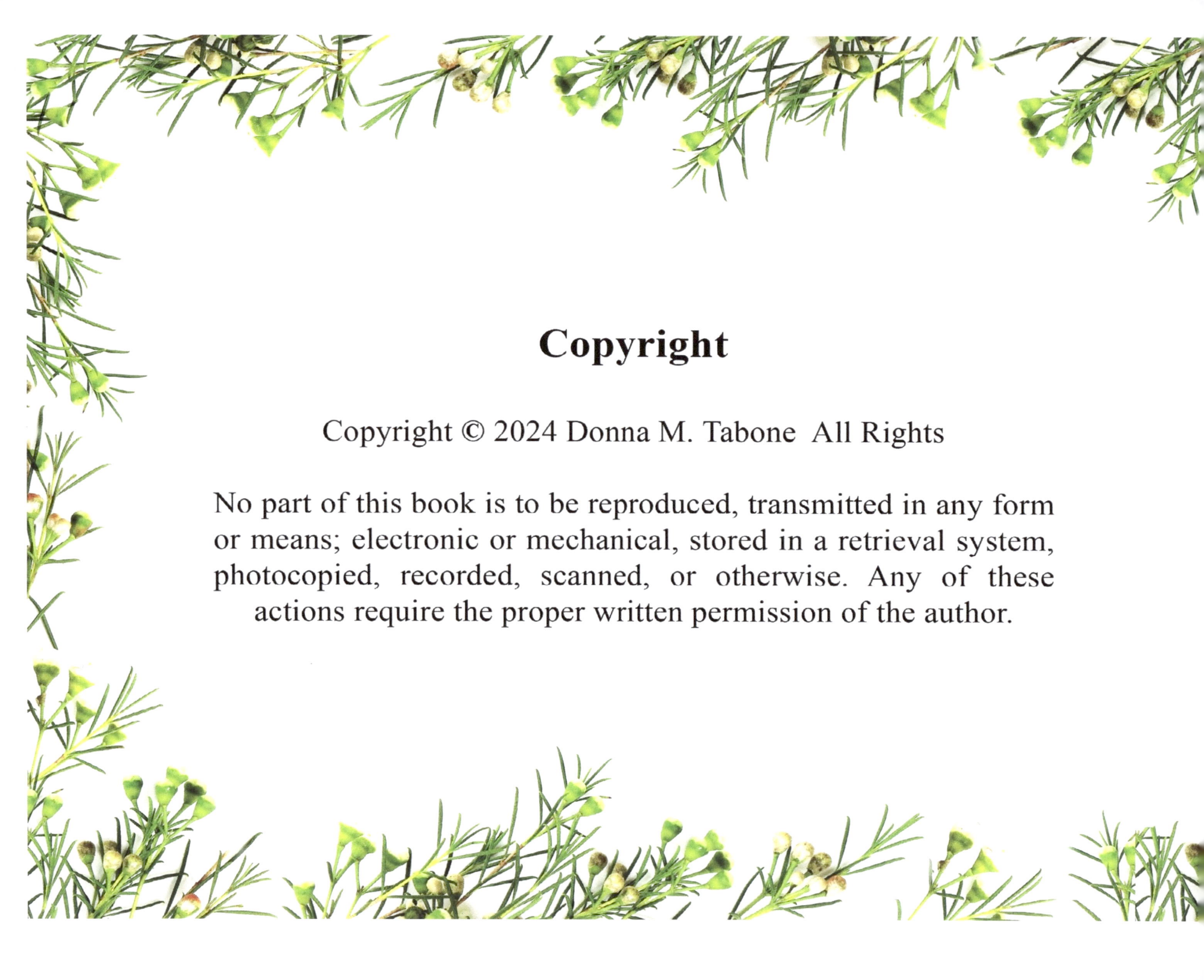

Copyright

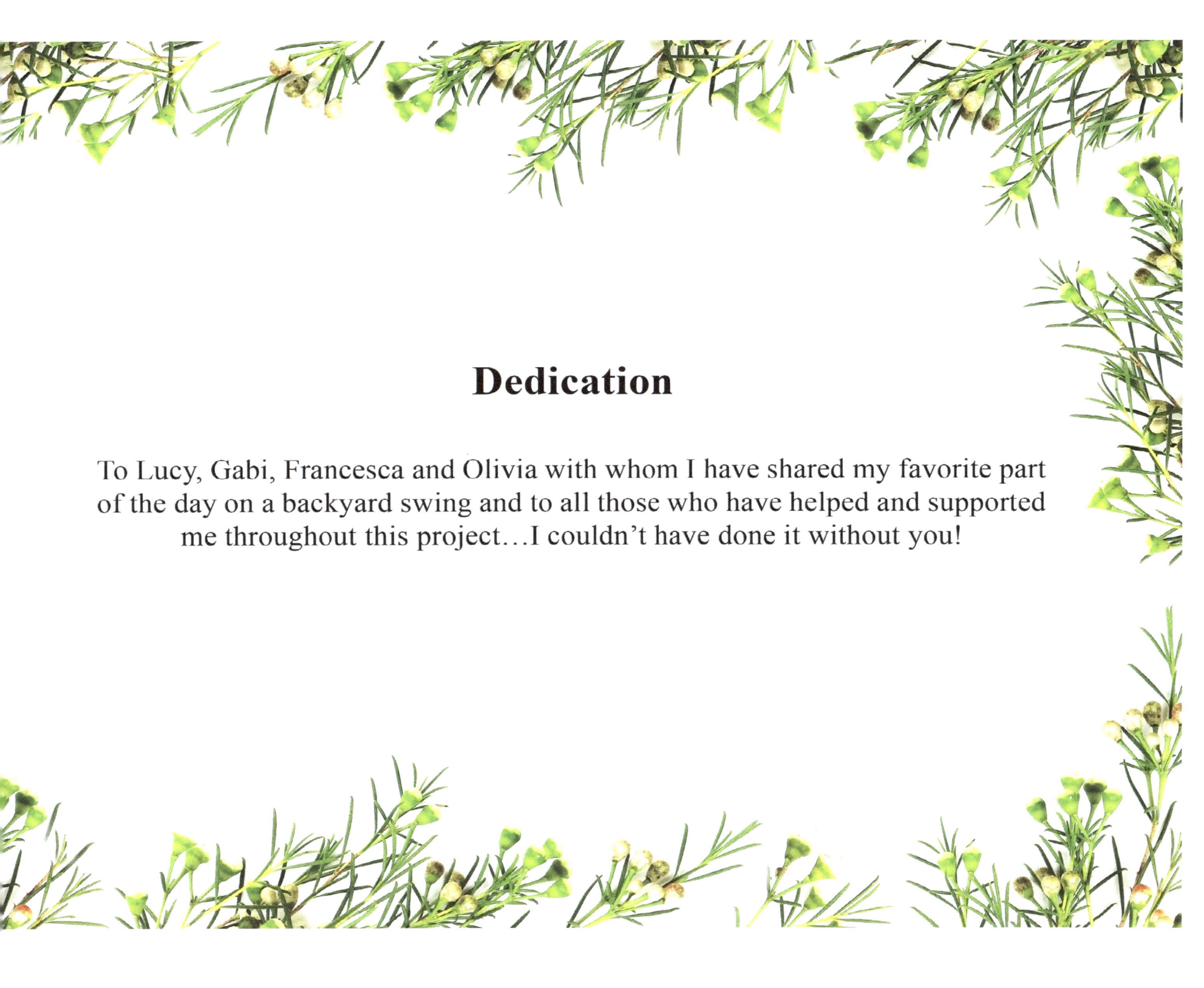

Dedication

To Lucy, Gabi, Francesca and Olivia with whom I have shared my favorite part of the day on a backyard swing and to all those who have helped and supported me throughout this project…I couldn't have done it without you!

When Sun hangs low in a pale blue sky,
and soft shadows appear under the dome,

when Nature slows its pace and all creatures
surrender,   Earth falls asleep.

Humming birds chitter among flowering shrubs,
flitting from blossom to blossom,

**sipping their last taste of nectar as
daylight fades.   Earth falls asleep.**

Bunnies savor a late meal of leaves and stems

before retiring to the safety of their burrows.
Earth falls asleep.

**Flowers tuck themselves inward,
away from the cool evening air,**

awaiting the warmth of a new day.
Earth falls asleep.

Gentle breezes creep in from the west,

nudging a windsock to dance its final steps.
Earth falls asleep.

**Tree branches gracefully sway
back and forth,**

**keeping time to an evening symphony bidding
farewell to the day. Earth falls asleep.**

**Crows trail across a dimly lit sky,
chasing after one another,**

dotting the horizon until they fade from view.
Earth falls asleep.

Silhouettes of mountain tops and tall
trees outline the open spaces,

capturing a quiet hush, signaling day's end.
Earth falls asleep.

**Mysterious moon, silvery white,
slivered and playful,**

grins mischievously at all creatures below!
Earth falls asleep.

Sun has set and a veil of stillness

shrouds all those in its path.
Earth falls asleep.

**When evening falls, all things under
the dome whisper**

a final "Good Night." Earth rests
until a new day begins…

And I am at peace, as Earth falls asleep.

www.ingramcontent.com/pod-product-compliance
Lightning Source LLC
Chambersburg PA
CBHW040814120626

46547CB00004B/546